# World Crafts and Recipes

## Recipe and Craft Guide to

# ISRAEL

### Laya Saul

## Mitchell Lane

P.O. Box 196
Hockessin, Delaware 19707
Visit us on the web: www.mitchelllane.com
Comments? email us: mitchelllane@mitchelllane.com

# Mitchell Lane
## PUBLISHERS

## World Crafts and Recipes

The Caribbean • China
France • India • Indonesia
**Israel** • Italy • Japan • South Africa

**PUBLISHER'S NOTE:** The facts on which this book is based have been thoroughly researched. Documentation of such research can be found on page 60. While every possible effort has been made to ensure accuracy, the publisher will not assume liability for damages caused by inaccuracies in the data, and makes no warranty on the accuracy of the information contained herein.

To reflect current usage, we have chosen to use the secular era designations BCE ("before the common era") and CE ("of the common era") instead of the traditional designations BC ("before Christ") and AD (*anno Domini*, "in the year of the Lord").

Special thanks to Tamar Ansh, author of the popular challah book *A Taste of Challah*, Feldheim Publishers, 2007, www.aTasteofChallah.com, and to Meira Davidson

The guttural sound that occurs in Hebrew can be represented in different ways in English. For this book the words that have that sound are represented as follows: *kh* or *ch*, which can be said with a hard *k* sound if the guttural is too hard to pronounce.

**Library of Congress**
Saul, Laya.
  Recipe and craft guide to Israel / by Laya Saul.
    p. cm. — (World crafts and recipes)
  Includes bibliographical references and index.
  ISBN 978-1-61228-081-3 (library bound)
  1. Cooking, Israeli—Juvenile literature.
  2. Handicraft—Israel—Juvenile literature.
  3. Cookbooks.  I. Title.
  TX360.I79S28 2012
  641.595694—dc23
                              2011031008

**eBook ISBN:** 9781612281681

**Printing**  1  2  3  4  5  6  7  8  9

PLB

# CONTENTS

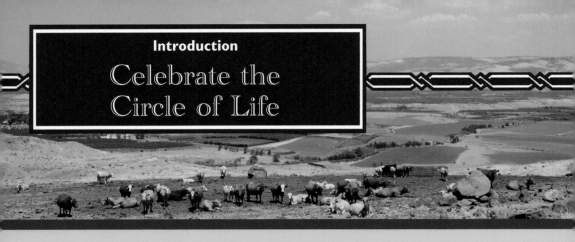

In a corner of Asia, and touching Egypt in Africa, is a region called the Middle East. On a sliver of land known to many as the Holy Land is a country that is full of passion, controversy, and spirituality. Israel is the homeland of the Jewish People. The holidays of Israel revolve around the Jewish calendar and reflect the seasons of life. They also mark the events and teachings of Jewish history as it is recorded in the Hebrew Bible, or Torah. The Hebrew calendar inspires the crafts and recipes in this book.

The civil calendar—January through December—is the most widely used calendar in the world. It is based on the sun, so it is also called a solar calendar. The Hebrew calendar is based on the sun and the moon, so the Jewish holidays don't always occur on the same days of the civil calendar. A leap year in the civil calendar occurs once every four years and adds one extra day. Most Hebrew calendar years have twelve months, but its cycle includes a leap year seven times every nineteen years and adds an extra month! That month is called Adar I, and it is added before the regular Adar (which for leap years becomes Adar II). In Israel, people use both calendars in everyday life.

King Solomon, known as one of the wisest men of all time, taught, "To every thing there is a season, and a time to every purpose under the heaven." This simple idea is also very deep. Everyone on this little blue planet we call Earth will have times when he or she will need to take things apart and times when he or she will build. There are times to cry and times to laugh. There are times to grieve and times to dance. The seasons of the year also bring with them the rhythm and pulse of life. There is a weekly cycle of work and rest (Shabbat); the monthly cycle from rebirth (the new moon at Rosh Chodesh) to celebration (biblical festivals fall on the full moon) and back again; and the yearly cycle, which starts with reflective New Year's festivities (Rosh Hashana) and days of atonement (Yom Kippur) and goes

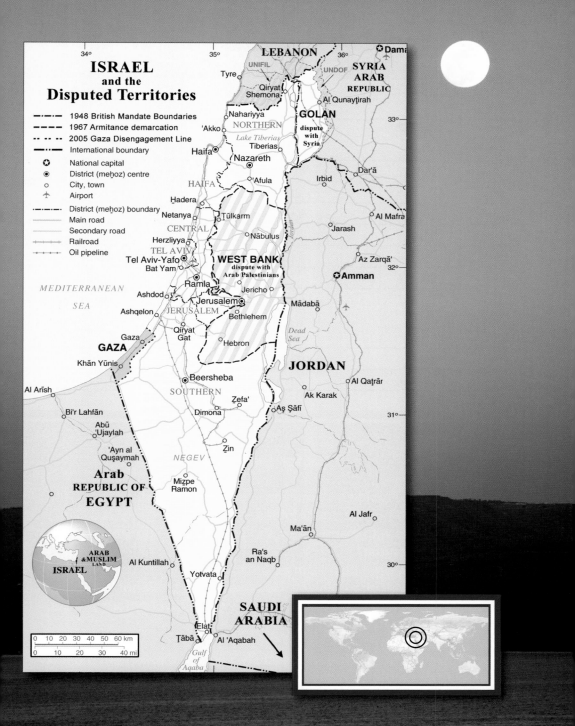

through Tu B'Av, the last full moon of the year, when people proclaim their love for one another and weddings abound. Whether solemn or mirthful, every holiday is a chance to celebrate in some way and to be with family

| Month | Holiday | Approximate Civil Month |
|---|---|---|
| Elul | Days of Awe Preparation | September |
| Tishrei | Rosh Hashana, Yom Kippur, Succot | October |
| Cheshvan | ——— | November |
| Kislev | Chanukah | December |
| Tevet | Asarah B'Tevet | January |
| Shvat | Tu B'Shvat | February |
| Adar | Purim | March |
| Nissan | Passover | April |
| Iyar | Yom Ha'atzmaut (Independence Day), Lag B'Omer | May |
| Sivan | Shavuot | June |
| Tammuz | 17th of Tammuz | July |
| Av | Tu B'Av | August |

## Tips for the Kitchen

Read through the recipe—all the way—before you start.

Wear an apron to protect your clothes.

Wash your hands with warm water and soap before you start and after handling raw meat.

Be careful! Always get help from an adult when you are using the oven, the stovetop, or sharp knives. Use oven mitts to lift hot lids, baking sheets, and pans. Protect the counter with a trivet before you set down a hot container.

Clean up right away.

Once you've made a recipe successfully, you can experiment the next time. Change the ingredients. Use cranberries instead of raisins, or honey instead of sugar.

Finally, share your food with your friends and family. Seeing people enjoy your cooking is as much fun as enjoying it yourself!

No matter where Jews live, they celebrate holidays with similar foods and traditions. The Torah outlines rules for eating, called  kosher laws (or kashrut), that all Jews must follow. While not everyone in Israel eats kosher, many Israelis do. Some of these laws are about which foods are forbidden, such as pork and shellfish, and which foods are permitted, such as beef and chicken. In a kosher kitchen, meat and dairy are not cooked together and they are not eaten at the same meal.

Israel is a small country with a warm climate just right for growing all kinds of fruits and vegetables that come to the kitchen ripe and fresh. And that is just perfect for preparing any festive meal!

Piles of colorful fruits and vegetables are available in markets called shuks, including this one in Tzfat, Israel.

# Rosh Hashana and Yom Kippur

The Hebrew month that precedes the Days of Awe is called Elul, and it usually falls around the month of September. Elul is a month to spiritually prepare for the Days of Awe, also known as the High Holy Days. At this time, Israel is buzzing with the preparation and excitement of new beginnings. It is the end of summer; children are beginning the new school year. Families shop for new clothes and shoes in preparation of the holiday season.

### ROSH HASHANA, JEWISH NEW YEAR

The Hebrew words for "New Year" are *Rosh Hashana* (RAHSH hah-SHAH-nah). *Rosh* means "head," so it literally means "the head of the year." We know that the way your head is facing can set the direction of the whole body. In the same way, Rosh Hashana is a time when people want to set their intentions and direction for the year ahead. The Jewish New Year, a two-day holiday, begins the first day of the Hebrew month of Tishrei (TEESH-ray). According to the Torah, Rosh Hashana is also the time that God will judge people and write in the Book of Life about the kind of year they will have. Therefore the Jewish New Year, while very joyful, is not a time for parties. Instead it's a time for looking inside, taking account of the year that passed, and apologizing for mistakes that hurt other people. Many people in Israel spend Rosh Hashana in a synagogue, in prayer, and enjoy a wonderful time with family at a festive meal. Flavorful dishes and treats abound.

One of the best-known traditions is to dip apple slices into honey. Apples symbolize the circle of life, and both the apple and the honey represent the sweetness and blessing we hope for in the coming year.

# Egg Challah with Raisins

All special holiday and Sabbath meals (see pages 52 to 57 for more about the Sabbath) begin with a blessing over a cup of wine or grape juice and then another blessing for bread. The traditional braided bread is called challah. Most of the year the bread is in the shape of a regular loaf, but on Rosh Hashana it is round to symbolize the circle of life. At this time of year, through all the Days of Awe, the bread is often sweetened with raisins, for a sweet year.

**Preparation Time:** About 2.5 hours, including rising and braiding
**Cooking Time:** 30 to 40 minutes
**Makes:** 3 small or 2 large challahs

## Ingredients
1/3 cup canola oil
1/2 cup sugar
1 1/2 cups warm water
1 ounce fresh yeast (or 2 1/2 to 3 teaspoons dry yeast)
6 cups sifted flour, plus a bit more if needed
3 medium eggs
1 3/4 teaspoons salt
1/2 to 1 cup golden raisins
Seeds of choice (such as poppy or sesame) or cinnamon sugar

## Instructions
1.  Pour the oil into a large mixing bowl and swirl it around.
2.  Add the sugar, warm water, and yeast. If you use fresh yeast, cover the bowl now with a towel or a plate and let the yeast activate.
3.  Add the sifted flour, 2 eggs, and salt. Using your hands or a mixer, knead the dough until it comes away from the sides of the bowl and is pliable and soft. (If the dough is too soft or sticky, add a little more flour and a few drops of oil. If the dough is too stiff, add a little more water and oil.)

## Israel Recipe

4. Knead the dough for another 2 minutes by hand. If it sticks, dust it with a little more flour.
5. Place it in an oiled large bowl, turn it over once or twice to oil all the sides, and cover the bowl loosely with plastic wrap or a clean dishtowel. Let the dough rise for 45 minutes to an hour, until it has doubled in size.
6. Punch the dough down, turn it over once or twice, and cover it again to rise for another 30 to 40 minutes.

7. Punch the dough down again. Divide the dough into two or three loaves, then divide each loaf into three or four strips.
8. Flatten each strip, sprinkle with raisins, then roll it up again with the raisins inside.
9. Braid each challah with three or four strands. You can keep it as a braided loaf, or you can

**TIP:** Challah can be frozen in freezer bags. Just defrost them about 4 hours before you want to use them.

tie the braid in a knot to make a round challah.

10. Line a baking tray with parchment paper and place the challahs on the tray. Cover them loosely with dishtowels. Let them rise until doubled, about 45 minutes.

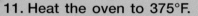

11. Heat the oven to 375°F.
12. Beat the remaining egg in a glass with a fork. Brush the egg on the challah loaves with a pastry brush. Sprinkle them with seeds, if you are using them, or with cinnamon sugar.
13. Bake for 15 minutes until the loaves start to brown, then turn down the heat to 350°F and finish baking, about 20 to 30 minutes. The challahs should be brown on top as well as on the bottom. They should sound hollow when you thump them with the back of a spoon.
14. Remove them from the oven and allow them to cool on a rack.

# Pomegranate Greeting Card

Artwork and decorations depicting pomegranates are common in Israel. Pomegranates are one of the seven species that are listed in the Bible as native to Israel. The others are wheat, barley, grapes, figs, olives, and dates.

At the Rosh Hashana meal, foods that have some kind of pun or symbolic meaning are eaten with a blessing. The puns are in Hebrew, of course, but here's an example in English. If you ate olives at the Rosh Hashana table, you could say, "May olive our prayers be answered." (May "all of" our prayers be answered.)

Pomegranates are a new fruit for the fall season, so they represent the New Year. These rich red fruits have many seeds, and the hope is that just as the pomegranate has hundreds of seeds, the New Year will bring each person the fulfillment of many mitzvot (MITZ-voht), or good deeds.

## Materials:

Light-colored construction paper
Markers
Red acrylic paint
Green ribbon (optional)
Cotton swabs
Paper plate

1. Fold the paper for the card in half.
2. Draw the shape of two pomegranate halves with a red marker. Notice the "crown" at the top of the fruit.
3. Paint over the outline with red paint.
4. Pour a small amount of red paint onto a paper plate. Dip a cotton swab into the paint and make one pomegranate seed at a time until the pomegranate halves are full.
5. When the paint is dry, use markers to draw sections around the seeds like a real pomegranate.
6. Tie a small green bow and place it on the top of the pomegranate if you like.
7. Inside the card, write a Rosh Hashana greeting, such as, "Have a sweet and good New Year!"

> **TIP: These pomegranate cards can also be hung in the Succah (see the next chapter).**

## YOM KIPPUR, DAY OF ATONEMENT

The days of Rosh Hashana are the first part of the Days of Awe. The days between Rosh Hashana and the last day of the ten days, called Yom Kippur, are supposed to be spent making sure there is peace within the community.

*Atonement* is a fancy word for "repairing." If a person hurt his friend, he has the chance to say he's sorry and to ask for forgiveness. It is also a time to give to those in need and to pray (talk with God). All of this is to prepare to stand before God on Yom Kippur with a clean slate. On Yom Kippur, people pray and apologize to God for the mistakes of the year. It is a day of spiritual purity, and many people wear white. It is considered the holiest day of the year.

Yom Kippur is a fasting day for adults—that means no eating or drinking from sunset on the eve of the holiday to after sunset the next day, around 25 hours. (Children who have not come of age and people who are ill do not fast.) There is a festive meal before the fast, and then a special meal to break the fast as well. Yom Kippur does not lend itself to a craft so much because the day is only about spirituality. After the fast is broken, there is a joy of entering the year with a fresh start. It is then that the preparations begin for the next holiday, Succot!

One of the happiest holidays, Succot (SOO-koht) lasts a whole week in early autumn. The Festival of Booths, as it is called in English, is written about in the Torah. God commanded the Jewish nation to observe this holiday. *"You shall celebrate this festival for God, seven days in the year, an eternal decree for your generations . . . you shall dwell in booths."* (Leviticus, chapter 23)

A Succah (SOO-kah) is a small hut that is built outside. It has between two and a half and four walls. The roof is made of branches that were cut or pruned from trees. The sky has to show through the branches, but the succah must have more shade than sun in the daytime. It's kind of like fancy camping in your yard for a week. Though most people don't actually

There are rituals associated with the succah, each with important symbolism. The most important ritual is the waving of the four species: branches from the willow, myrtle, and palm (lulov), along with an etrog, or citron (part of the citrus family, it looks like a large lemon). This ritual is a commandment also. If even one of the four species is missing, the mitzvah is not complete. Waving the four species together represents the unity of the nation.

sleep in the succah, meals are eaten there and family and friends spend time together there. One teaching says that being in a succah is like getting a hug from God.

In Israel, it seems as if the whole country is on vacation for the week of Succot. Many people travel, and festivals abound. Even restaurants build succahs outside for their customers. Foods for this festival celebrate the harvest. Dishes that use several types of fresh fruits and vegetables symbolize the blessings of a plentiful harvest.

# Sweet Potato Tzimmes

**Preparation Time:** 15 minutes
**Cooking Time:** 25–35 minutes
**Serves:** 8

Tzimmes is a traditional sweet side dish originating from the Eastern European Jews. It is eaten at Succot and at other holiday meals, including Rosh Hashana and Passover. Some families serve it at other times of the year as well, as a side dish with beef or as a main dish. It can be made with honey, but apple or orange juice will also make it sweet.

## Ingredients
4–5 cups of diced sweet potatoes
6 dried plums, pitted and
  chopped
6 dried apricots, chopped
2 carrots, chopped
½ teaspoon cinnamon
1 cup apple OR orange juice

## Instructions
1. Put all ingredients in a pot.
2. Cook for about a half hour, until the sweet potatoes are soft, stirring occasionally; add more juice as needed to keep it moist.
3. Serve as a side dish.

## Ingredients

Crackers—whole wheat or graham
Stick pretzels or breadsticks for the top
Marshmallow fluff or peanut butter
Paper plate
Variety of small candy decorations used for cupcakes
Any small-leaf edible greenery, such as celery tops, parsley, or basil

## Instructions

1.  Using crackers and marshmallow fluff or peanut butter as "glue," build three sides of a four-sided hut. Use sparingly or the succah will be too heavy. You can also use some fluff to anchor the base of the succah.
2.  Lay the breadsticks or pretzels across the top.
3.  Place small sprigs of parsley or other edible, leafy vegetable across the roof pieces.
4.  Gently decorate the top of the succah or the plate with tiny candies to look like lights or fruits.

# Chanukah

Chanukah is a bright holiday of lighting candles, eating special foods, singing songs, and telling the story of the Maccabees. Also known as the Festival of Light, Chanukah lasts for eight nights and days. A Chanukah menorah (men-OR-ah), also called a chanukiah (chan-oo-KEY-ah), is a candelabra with nine branches: one branch for each night plus a helper candle (called a shamash) that lights all the others. On the first night of Chanukah, the shamash plus one light is lit. On the second night the shamash and two are lit, and so on until the eighth night when all the candles are lit.

At the time of the destruction of the First Temple in 425 BCE, the Syrian Greeks made it illegal for Jews to practice their faith. They tried to force the Jews to practice idolatry (bowing down to and worshiping statues), which is against their faith. The Maccabee family was loyal to God. Against all odds, they rose up and fought against the strong empire to regain their freedom. Eventually the Jews took back control of the Holy Temple. As the original menorah was going to be lit, they searched for the special, pure olive oil that would be the fuel for the lights. They found just enough oil to light the menorah for one day, but it would take a week to make more. Miraculously, the oil stayed lit for eight days!

Chanukah comes at the darkest time of the year. That's a time when we need encouragement to remember that even though it may be dark now, we can make the world a brighter place with our good actions. When families light their own Chanukah menorahs, they place them either outside in special glass cases or in the window. This is to remember that light is meant to be shared! It is fun to walk through neighborhoods all around Israel and see the simple yet meaningful lights.

A game using a four-sided spinning top called a *sevivon* (seh-vee-VOHN) or a dreidel (DRAY-del) is played. On each side of the top is a letter, and these letters represent the phrase, "A great miracle happened here." (Outside of Israel, one letter is different, and the phrase is "A great miracle happened there.") During the rule of the Syrian Greeks, it was against the law to learn Torah. Young men who were learning Torah in defiance would study anyway. If a soldier came to arrest them, they would pretend they were only playing this game.

# Potato Pancakes: Levivot, or Latkes

The miracle of Chanukah involved oil, so it is traditional to eat foods that are fried in oil for this holiday. The most popular are potato pancakes, known as levivot (leh-vee-VOHT) or latkes (LOT-kiss), and sufganiyot (soof-gah-nee-OHT), which are jelly doughnuts. Many people like to eat potato pancakes with sour cream, applesauce, or both.

**Preparation Time:** 20 minutes
**Cooking Time:** Approximately 12 minutes
**Serves:** 4–6

## Ingredients:

Oil for frying
4–6 large potatoes
1 large onion
2 eggs, slightly beaten
¼ cup matzah meal or 3 tablespoons flour
1 teaspoon salt
Pepper to taste

> **TIP:** Substitute or add grated zucchini, sweet potato, or other vegetables for the potatoes.

## Instructions:

1. Grate potatoes and onions with a grater (or in a food processor). Drain them in a colander while preparing the other ingredients.
2. Add the eggs, matzah meal, salt, and pepper and mix well.

3. In a large frying pan or skillet, heat oil for frying.
4. Place a heaping tablespoon of the potato batter in the oil and flatten it with the back of a spatula.

5. Cook until it is golden brown and then flip to cook the other side.
6. Remove the pancake from the pan and let it drain on a plate lined with paper towels.
7. Serve warm.

# Felt Menorah

The word *Chanukah* comes from the Hebrew word that means "to dedicate." The Chanukah miracle happened when the Jews went to rededicate the menorah and Temple to the service of God. Chanukah also has the word "to educate" in its root. So Chanukah is an important time to educate and remind children that each person makes a difference and brings light to the world. Many families light just one menorah for the whole family. In many other families each family member has his or her own menorah to light. Some families use pure olive oil with a cotton wick just like in the days of the Temple. Other families use brightly colored candles. No matter what the tradition, there is always bright light that is enjoyed just for the pleasure of the light itself!

## Materials:

Pencil or fabric marker
Gold or yellow felt
Brightly colored felt
Scissors
Glue
Dark felt for the
    background
Small Velcro dots

## Instructions:

1.  On the gold felt, draw the shape of the menorah. It should have eight places for candles that are at the same level, then one that is higher than the rest. Cut it out.

2. Cut out nine slender rectangles for the candles from bright-colored felt, and nine flames from the gold felt.
3. Glue the flames to the candles.
4. Glue the menorah to the big piece of felt, and then fix the Velcro dots in place so that you can add one felt candle each night.

## BIRTHDAY OF TREES
# Tu B'Shvat

On day 15 (Tu) of the Hebrew month of Shvat, when the moon is full, is the holiday whose name is the date (like the Fourth of July in the United States). Tu B'Shvat is the day that the trees are honored. The holiday falls around February of the civil calendar. In Israel, most of the winter rains have fallen. The trees are beginning to wake up from their winter slumber as the sap within begins to rise. The first trees that blossom across the Israeli countryside are the almond trees with their delicate pink flowers.

Before Tu B'shvat, all across the country, grocery stores prepare for the holiday by stocking dried fruits, nuts, and unusual fresh fruits, such as star fruit and passion fruit. Many families and schools hold a Tu B'Shvat seder (SAY-der), which is a light meal. A table is set with fruits and nuts from trees that grow in Israel, and they will be blessed to honor and give thanks for the trees. Tu B'Shvat is also when thousands of people go into the fields to plant new trees.

Forestry is an important part of Israel's relationship with the land. Forests are not native to Israel, but over the decades since 1948, when the Jews returned from their 2,000-year exile, over 240 million trees have been planted.

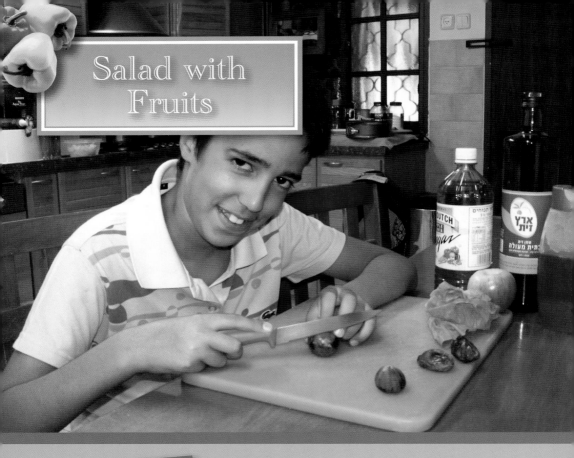

# Salad with Fruits

## Ingredients:

5 cups lettuce, torn into bite-sized pieces
¼ cup figs, dried or fresh, chopped
¼ cup pomegranate seeds
¼ cup dried dates, chopped
¼ to ⅓ cups seedless grapes, cut in half
⅓ cup apples, cut into bite-sized pieces
Optional: raisins, dried cranberries, Clementine segments,
    or other fruits that you like
2–3 tablespoons olive oil
3 tablespoons orange juice
2 tablespoons lemon juice (optional)
2 tablespoons apple cider vinegar
2 tablespoons honey
salt and pepper to taste
poppyseeds (optional)

1. In a large bowl, gently mix the lettuce and all the fruit.
2. In another bowl, mix the liquid ingredients and, if you'd like, salt and pepper. Pour the mixture over the fruit.
3. Toss the salad well.
4. If you'd like, sprinkle the salad with poppyseeds.

This simple but exotic salad is also nice to serve at Rosh Hashana, when people like to bless and eat the new fruits of the season.

# Tissue Tree

## Materials:

Colored tissue paper (brown, green, pink)
One piece of construction paper
New pencil with good eraser
Scissors
Glue
Paper plate for glue

## Instructions:

1. Draw a tree. Make sure there is a trunk and at least four branches. Add only scribbles where you want the leaves to appear.
2. Cut squares of tissue that are about 1 inch by 1 inch. First cut 1-inch-wide strips, then layer the strips to cut the squares from them. You will need about 100 squares for the leaves and 50 to 75 for the trunk.
3. Take one square at a time. Wrap it around the end of the pencil covering the eraser. The tissue paper will be the shape of the pencil eraser now. Keep it on the pencil, and then dip it in the glue.

4. Carefully place the glued end of the tissue paper on your drawn tree.
5. Do this for each piece of tissue paper until you have covered your tree. Let the glue dry.

## THINGS AREN'T ALWAYS AS THEY SEEM
# Purim

Purim celebrates the biblical book of Esther. In that story, the Persian King Xerxes (Ahasuerus) searches for a new queen. He chooses a Jewess named Esther who does *not* tell him she is a Jew. Her uncle Mordechai is the leader of the Jews and sits outside the palace to be near his niece. The king's top man, Haman, wants power and tells everyone to bow to him. Mordechai refuses to bow to the evil Haman, so Haman brings a plan to the king to kill all the Jews.

The word *Purim* means "lots." Lots are a way to choose something; it's where the word *lottery* comes from. The "lots" in this story were used to choose the date that all the Jews would be killed. In the story, there are many coincidences and turns of events that save the Jews—including how Mordechai saves the king's life. Haman is revealed as the bad guy, and in the end, the Jews are allowed to defend themselves and are not murdered.

*Esther Denouncing Haman,* Ernest Normand, c. 1915

From this story come the customs of the holiday of Purim. The story is read from a handwritten scroll in homes and synagogues. Sometimes people make plays of the story. Because the story has so many twists and turns, we see that things are not always as they seem.

Purim is a favorite holiday of young and old alike. It's a time of joy and sharing. The sharing of gift baskets (in Hebrew called *mishoakh manot*) gives people who have been mad at each other an opportunity to make up. At schools, there is a day of carnival games and prizes, and many people wear costumes. People begin singing Purim songs at the start of the Hebrew month of Adar. One perky song says, "Whoever enters the month of Adar will have multiplied joy!" It is not unusual for a class to be interrupted with a song. Instead of the teacher getting angry, he or she will join in with the spontaneous singing and dancing.

# Hamantaschen

Gragger

This jelly-filled pastry cookie, whose name means "Haman's hat," delights Israelis every spring when it's time for the holiday of Purim. It symbolizes the defeat of the evil Haman. The gragger is used every time Haman's name is mentioned during the reading of the story. Because Haman persecuted the Jews, his name is supposed to be drowned out by noise. The following family recipe is over 100 years old. Be creative. You can add almond extract to the dough or use any kind of pie filling or preserves that you like.

## Ingredients

3 eggs
½ cup sugar
Pinch salt
½ cup oil
¼ cup water (or orange juice)
2½ cups flour plus 1 cup and more as needed
2 rounded teaspoons of baking powder (make sure they are mixed well)
Jam or other filling

**Preparation Time:** 24 minutes
**Cooking Time:** 12–15 minutes
**Serves:** 12–15

## Instructions

1. In a bowl, mix together the eggs, sugar, salt, oil, and water (or orange juice).
2. Stir the baking powder into the 2½ cups flour, then add them to the bowl of liquids. Mix with a spoon. (It will still be loose.)
3. Put one cup of flour on the cutting board, then dump the dough in the middle and knead

lightly. When you feel it is enough (not too firm), separate the dough into four pieces.

4. Roll out each piece, adding more flour if it sticks. Use a 3-inch cookie cutter or the edge of a drinking glass to make round pieces.

5. Add ½ teaspoon of filling to the center of each circle of dough, then pinch the edges together in three places to form a triangle. It should be a little open in the middle to show the filling.

6. Bake at 350°F for about 15 minutes until light golden brown.
7. Optional: Dust with powdered sugar when cooled.

# Make a Mask

## Materials:

Plain paper
Pencil
Colored card stock or colorful plastic page dividers
Glue
Scissors
Glitter, sequins, feathers, die-cut foam shapes
Large rubber band or wooden dowel, 10 to 12 inches long
Hole punch

## Instructions:

1. Have **an adult** use a plain sheet of paper to make a mask stencil for your face, keeping the nose free. Have the adult locate where you need to cut for your eyes.
2. Trace around this stencil on the card stock.
3. Cut out the mask, including holes for the eyes.
4. Decorate with sequins, glitter, feathers, and other fun pieces.

5. After the glue dries, poke a small hole on each side of the mask with a pencil or hole punch. The best place to make the holes for the rubber bands (so the mask will stay on well) is at the edge of the mask in line with the eye holes. Cut a rubber band and thread it through each hole. Knot the ends and tape over the knots on the inside of the mask for strength.

Instead of a rubber band, you can use a wooden dowel. Glue it on one side of the mask and use it as a handle to hold it up to your face.

# Passover

The well-known holiday of freedom is called Passover. It is celebrated in the spring in the Hebrew month of Nissan (NEE-sahn), which comes from the Hebrew word meaning "miracles." In Hebrew, Passover is called Pesach (PAY-sakh). Passover is celebrated for a whole week. In biblical times, the Egyptians enslaved the Jews and made them suffer. The story of Passover, finding freedom from the bitter slavery, is full of miracles and drama—so much that movies have been made about it. When the Israelites left Egypt, they had to leave very quickly and did not have time for their bread to rise, so they made flat bread called matzah that is like a kind of cracker. As hundreds of thousands of Israelites left Egypt, the Egyptian army followed them and a miracle happened: the Red Sea split apart, allowing them to cross. They traveled toward the Land of Israel, the Promised Land, by way of the Sinai Desert, where they received the Ten Commandments from God at Mount Sinai.

On the first night of this holiday is a special meal called a seder. A Passover Seder involves telling the story of the Jews leaving the slavery of Egypt and other important teachings. Symbolic foods are arranged on a plate: bitter herbs represent slavery; charoset, a mixture of nuts, cinnamon, and wine, represents the mortar the Jews used while making Egyptian buildings; a vegetable such as a potato dipped in salt water represents tears; a piece of meat or bone represents the Passover sacrifice at the Temple; and a hard-boiled egg symbolizes a festival offering. (Outside of Israel, Jewish families observe two nights of seders.)

The Haggadah (hah-gah-DAH) is the short book from which families read at the seder. It describes the symbols and stories of Passover. Within the laws and traditions, each family has its own way of celebrating the seder depending on where they are from and whether they have young children at the table. The idea is to make sure the story is taught in every generation. Every Jew is supposed to feel as if he or she were personally taken out of slavery. The Jewish people have celebrated Passover every year beginning with the year it actually happened over 3,300 years ago!

During this holiday, instead of eating regular bread, matzah is eaten, and all things leavened are forbidden. A traditional food enjoyed at many Passover Seders is matzah ball soup. Matzah balls are like dumplings.

# Matzah Ball Soup

Ingredients:

**Matzah Balls:**
4 eggs
1 teaspoon of salt
4 tablespoons of oil
4 tablespoons of cold water
1 cup matzah meal (fine matzah crumbs)
2 quarts of water plus 1 teaspoon of salt
    for cooking the matzah balls

**Soup:**
5 quarts of water
3–4 medium onions
2 stalks of celery with the leaves
1–2 carrots, cut up
1 small parsnip, peeled
1 tablespoon of olive oil
¼ teaspoon turmeric
1 teaspoon dill and/or
    1 teaspoon parsley
Salt and pepper to taste
Dash of cayenne pepper (optional)

**Preparation Time:** 25 minutes
plus 2 hours or overnight
**Cooking Time:** 90 minutes
**Serves:** 12

38

1. Put eggs, oil, salt, and cold water in a mixing bowl and lightly beat the eggs. Then add the matzah meal and gently stir together until just mixed. Cover the bowl and place it in the refrigerator for two hours or overnight.
2. When you are ready to cook the matzah balls: Boil 2 quarts of water and 1 teaspoon of salt in a pot. Scoop a heaping tablespoon of the dough and gently shape it into a ball. (The less you handle it the nicer it will turn out.) Put the balls into the water. They will sink to the bottom, but as they cook, they will nearly double in size and float to the top.
3. Simmer on low for about 35 minutes, then let them sit for another 5 to 10 minutes. Remove them with a slotted spoon so they can drain, then place them in a bowl.
4. To make the soup, put the rest of the ingredients into a stockpot and bring to a boil. Simmer until the vegetables are tender. Celery leaves may be removed at this point or served.
5. Fifteen minutes before you serve the soup, add the matzah balls and heat them. Serve and enjoy.

# Elijah's Cup

At every Passover Seder, an extra cup of wine or grape juice is put on the table for the prophet Elijah. Tradition says that Elijah will herald the coming of the messiah, the person who will be anointed as a king over Israel. When that happens, there will be peace on earth. Near the end of the Passover Seder, the door is opened to invite the spirit of Elijah, who will usher in a time of great peace in the world.

## Materials:

Plastic or glass wine goblet
Glue
Beads and/or other decorations, such as stickers, puff paint, tissue paper, glitter glue, sequins, and decorative gems

## Instructions:

1. Choose the colors and design you like and decorate the goblet. You could choose a theme like flowers, fruits, or rainbows, or items from the seder plate.
2. Be sure to allow for enough drying time.

## INDEPENDENCE DAY
# Yom Ha'atzmaut

After the destruction of the second Temple in Jerusalem, the people of the nation of Israel were exiled, scattered to other countries as their land was taken over by the Roman Empire. For 2,000 years the Jews prayed to return to the Holy Land. During World War II there was much devastation. By the end of the war, Adolf Hitler and the Nazi regime had murdered six million Jews. After the war the United Nations officially gave some land (in British-ruled Palestine) for a Jewish State that would be Israel. Independence Day was May 14, 1948.

The little nation was not to rebuild in peace: its Arab neighbors immediately attacked those who came to build the new state. Through miracles and wonder, Israel won that War of Independence and celebrates every year in much the same way as the Fourth of July is celebrated in the United States: with flags, fireworks, and barbecues. In Israel, Memorial Day is the day before Independence Day. The fallen soldiers are remembered with love for their part in the freedom of the land. Just as the religious holidays begin at sunset and end the following day after sunset, Independence Day begins the night before with a blaze of fireworks.

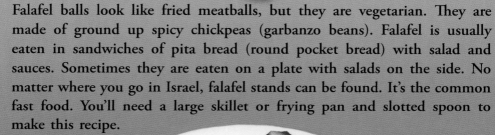

# Falafel

Falafel balls look like fried meatballs, but they are vegetarian. They are made of ground up spicy chickpeas (garbanzo beans). Falafel is usually eaten in sandwiches of pita bread (round pocket bread) with salad and sauces. Sometimes they are eaten on a plate with salads on the side. No matter where you go in Israel, falafel stands can be found. It's the common fast food. You'll need a large skillet or frying pan and slotted spoon to make this recipe.

15-ounce can of garbanzo beans (chickpeas), drained
1 medium onion chopped (or pureed in food processor)
1 clove of garlic, minced
2 teaspoons dried parsley
½ teaspoon cumin
½ teaspoon salt
2 tablespoons flour
Oil for frying
Hummus or tahini
Pita bread
Lettuce, raw onions, tomatoes, cucumbers, according to taste
Spicy sauce, such as hot pepper sauce (optional)

**Preparation Time:** 10–20 minutes
**Cooking Time:** About 5 minutes
**Serves:** 3–4

## Instructions:

1. Combine beans, onion, garlic, spices, and flour in a food processor. Mix until you have a thick paste. (If you don't have a food processor, you can mash everything together with a fork.)
2. Form into small meatball-size balls and fry until golden brown (about 2 to 5 minutes).
3. Serve with hummus or tahini and cut-up veggies in pita bread. Drizzle with spicy sauce if you'd like.

# Mizrach Wall Hanging

מזרח

*"From the rising of the sun unto the going down thereof, the Lord's name is to be praised."* ~Psalm 113:3

Jews the world over face Jerusalem to pray. From the United States, they turn to the east, which is *mizrach* (MEEZ-rahk) in Hebrew. *Mizrach* comes from the word "to shine." East is the direction from which the sun shines each morning.

## Materials:

Ready-made plaques from the craft store
Old newspapers
Pencils
Markers
Fabric or puff paint
Glitter, decorative gems
Glue
Raffia
Beads (optional)

1. Cover your work area with old newspapers.
2. Draw your letters that say either "Mizrach" or "East" onto the plaque in pencil. Then draw the design you want around the letters.
3. Carefully trace each letter with marker or fabric paint.
4. Decorate the rest of your plaque with colors and textures that you love. Include bright colors and fancy shapes.

5. When the paint and glue are dry, string raffia through the holes in the plaque. You can string beads to raffia on the top where it will hang or even add a fringe or beads (if there are holes) at the bottom of the plaque.
6. Display your mizrach plaque on an eastern wall.

# RECEIVING THE TORAH
## Shavuot

In early summer, counting exactly fifty days from the second night of Passover, is the festival called Shavuot (shah-voo-OHT). The Hebrew word *Shavuot* literally means "weeks." (There are seven weeks between Passover and Shavuot.) Shavuot celebrates the anniversary of God giving the Torah to the Jewish people.

God instructed Moses—who was the leader of the Jews—to climb Mount Sinai and receive the Torah. Moses brought down two sapphire stone tablets that had the Ten Commandments inscribed on them. The Jews agreed to receive and act according to the teachings. It is a gift for all generations. During the times of the Temple, the Jews in the Land of Israel would bring the first fruits of their crops to the Temple to give to the High Priests, called Cohenim. Think of a big road trip of tens of thousands of people and a big party in Jerusalem!

The tradition every year since then is to stay up all night and learn from the teachings of the Torah. There are two other customs for Shavuot. One is to decorate the synagogue and the home with flowers and greens. This is because it is told that when the Torah was given at Sinai, the base of the mountain was covered with flowers and greens. The other custom is to eat foods that are dairy, and cheesecake has become a popular choice for this holiday.

# No Bake Cheesecake

**Crust:**
6 whole graham crackers or 12–15 shortbread cookies
6 tablespoons butter

**Filling:**
16 ounces cream cheese
8 ounces sour cream or whipped cream
½ cup confectioners' sugar
1 teaspoon vanilla
1 tablespoon lemon juice
Fresh berries of your choice (optional)

**Preparation Time**
**Crust:** 5 minutes
**Filling:** 10 minutes
**Refrigerate:** 3 hours

## Instructions:

1. Put the crackers or cookies in a heavy plastic zipper bag and pound or roll them gently but firmly until they are crumbs.
2. Melt the butter and mix in the crumbs.
3. Press the mixture firmly into an 8-inch pie pan or spring form pan and refrigerate.
4. Mix the filling ingredients well (by hand or with a mixer). Spoon it into the piecrust shell and smooth it out with a spatula.
5. Top with fresh berries of your choice.
6. Chill for a few hours so it can set.
7. Serve and enjoy!

# Magazine Flowers

Magazines to cut up
Pencil
Scissors
Glue stick
Paper fasteners
Round objects of different sizes (plastic lids, CDs, cups)

## Instructions:

1. Using bright pages from the magazines, draw circles using different-sized templates and cut them out.
2. Fold each circle in half and then half again and cut different shapes at the edge. You can cut spiky or curved or zigzag, as you would for paper snowflakes.

   **IMPORTANT: Do not cut the center point.**

3. Put the smallest circle on the paper fastener, then add the bigger ones.
4. For the stem, roll a page from the magazine and glue it together.
5. With the scissors, make a small cut in the top of the stem and put the fastener through the opening and fasten in place. (You can add a piece of tape to make it more secure.)
6. Put your flowers in a pretty vase.

It is written in the Torah that in six days God created the universe and on the seventh day He rested. God named the seventh day the Sabbath. When the Jews were freed from the slavery of Egypt, God commanded them to take the Sabbath as a day of rest—a day that they would refrain from doing work, including cooking and even lighting a fire. Every week many homes honor the day with festive meals served on white tablecloths, and by lighting candles on Friday night just before the Sabbath begins. Bread, salads, fish, and sometimes soup are served.

In Israel, the weekend is really only Saturday, the Sabbath day. Not everyone in Israel observes the Sabbath in a religious way, but those who do go to the synagogue to pray. When they come home they eat special foods and sing songs. A Sabbath meal always begins with a blessing over wine. Then there is a blessing over bread—the challah that is on page 9. During the year, the braided challah is in the shape of a loaf (and usually does not have raisins). During the large Friday night meal, the whole family "welcomes" the Sabbath with song as if it were an honored queen. Then on Saturday for lunch is another big meal. Many homes serve a kind of stew called cholent with this lunch.

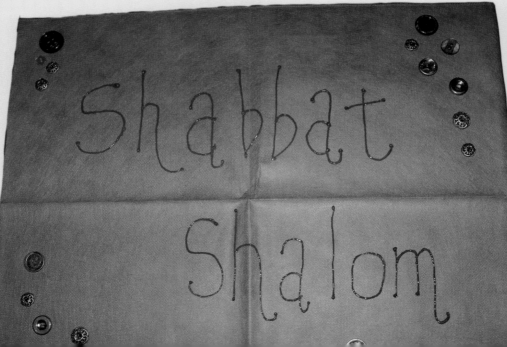

It is commonly understood that between 2 o'clock in the afternoon until 4 o'clock in the afternoon is quiet time because so many people like to nap on the Sabbath. After the quiet time, the happy sound of kids at play rings through the air.

# Cholent

Because lighting a fire (including turning on a stove) is prohibited on the Sabbath, many families put on a pot of stew on Friday afternoon. It continues to cook slowly overnight and is ready to eat on Saturday for Shabbat lunch. The recipes can vary, depending on whether the cook is Sephardic or Ashkenazic. Cholent can be really anything that sounds good to the cook, something that the family will enjoy. This recipe is a variation of a traditional Ashkenazi cholent. More ideas on how to vary this recipe are below.

**Preparation Time:**
   25 minutes
**Cooking Time:** Overnight
**Serves:** 8

## Ingredients:

*In a slow cooker:*
1 tablespoon oil
2 onions, cut up
1 pound beef, cut into cubes
½ pound potatoes, cubed
2 carrots, cut up
2 stalks celery, cut up
1 small green or red pepper, chopped
1 tablespoon salt
¼ teaspoon black pepper

Optional (add any or all of these to your taste): ¼ teaspoon cayenne pepper, bay leaf, chopped tomato or tomato sauce, garlic, ½ cup barley, 1 cup kidney or white beans (either from a can or boiled first for 10 minutes—do not cook dried beans in a slow cooker without washing and then boiling them first for at least 10 minutes)

1.  Rub the bottom of the slow cooker with oil. Put all the rest of the ingredients except salt and tomato into the slow cooker and stir. Cover with water.
2.  Cook on the high setting until bubbles start to form, then turn the slow cooker to the lowest setting. Stir in salt and tomatoes, and let it cook overnight.
3.  Serve hot with challah.

The Gathering of Manna,
Musée de la Chartreuse,
1460–1470

After the Israelites left the slavery of Egypt, they wandered in the desert for 40 years. During those years, God provided them every day with a type of food called manna, which they gathered from the morning dew. At the Shabbat table, the tablecloth below the bread and the cover on top of it are reminders of that gift.

## Materials:

Old newspapers
Fabric, minimum 24 inches by 30 inches
Masking tape
Paper and pencils to plan
Fabric paint
Lace edging or other material to finish sides
Glue gun

> TIP: Avoid glitter glue or other small decorative pieces that could get into the food on the Shabbat table.

## Instructions:

1. Cover your work area with old newspapers. Tape the fabric tightly to the newspapers so that the fabric paint will not run.
2. Plan your project using pencil and paper first. Practice any lettering on the paper, and keep the design simple.
3. When you like what you have, redraw your design on the fabric, then paint it with the fabric paint. Use small amounts of paint so that it doesn't run.
4. When the fabric paint is dry, use the glue gun to hot-glue borders or lace or other finishing touches to the edges of the cover.

## NEW START—ROSH CHODESH
# Spicy Fish

The first day of each Hebrew month is called Rosh Chodesh (RAHSH KHOH-desh). The new month begins with a new moon—when the moon is at its smallest, little sliver. From then it will wax into a full moon, which is always in the middle of the Hebrew month. The word *chodesh* comes from the word that means "new," and it reminds us that every month is a chance to renew and start fresh. There is also a beautiful idea that while the moon is just a sliver and its moonlight is not really seen, we still know that the moon is whole. We can use that idea to think about the hard times in life. In dark times, the light is really still there, even if we don't see it. Rosh Chodesh is a gentle holiday that comes each month to renew the spirit. There are no additional laws for the day, but there are customs, such as dressing a little nicer—and women may refrain from regular housework. The newness of Rosh Chodesh—like the newness of Rosh Hashana—brings continual hope for a bright and good life.

The cultures of the Eastern European countries that hosted the Jews while they were in exile, and the produce that was available there, influenced some of the dishes in this book. Other flavors arrived with the nearly 600,000 Jews who moved to Israel from the surrounding Arab countries after the War of Independence. With Israel's miles and miles of coastline on the Mediterranean Sea, its cuisine also includes many seafood dishes. The author's neighbor, whose parents immigrated to Israel from the Arab country of Tunisia, inspired this recipe for spicy fish.

## Ingredients:

2 medium onions, peeled and sliced
2 medium tomatoes, cut into chunks
1 red pepper, seeded and sliced
2–4 cloves of garlic, chopped
Sprinkle of salt, pepper, turmeric,
    cumin, cayenne pepper (this is spicy
    hot so use only a little
    bit), and dill
Any fish filets, such as whitefish,
    tuna, or salmon, enough
    to fit into a 12-inch skillet (with a lid)
Olive (or other vegetable) oil

## Instructions:

1. Place the onions on the bottom of the skillet.
2. Sprinkle the tomatoes, peppers, and garlic evenly on the onions.
3. Sprinkle the spices lightly onto the fish, then spread the fish on top of the vegetables.
4. Drizzle olive oil over the fish.
5. Cover the skillet and cook over medium heat until the fish is cooked (approximately 40 minutes). You will know it's done when it flakes with a fork.
6. Serve warm or cold.

# Further Reading

**Books**

Hintz, Martin. *Israel: Enchantment of the World*. Second Edition. Danbury, CT: Children's Press, 2006.

Saul, Laya. *We Visit Israel*. Hockessin, DE: Mitchell Lane Publishers, 2012.

Young, Emma. *National Geographic's Countries of the World: Israel*. Washington, DC: National Geographic Children's Books, 2008.

**Works Consulted**

This book is based on the author's years living in Israel as the mother of an Orthodox Jewish family, and on the following sources:

Ansh, Tamar. *A Taste of Challah*. Nanuet, NY: Feldheim Publishers, 2007. http://www.aTasteofChallah.com

Chabad. "Tu B'Shevat: The New Year for Trees." http://www.chabad.org/library/article_cdo/aid/3264/jewish/Tu-BShevat.htm

Jewish National Fund. "The Recovery of Northern Israel Through a Forest's Eyes." Press Release, January 3, 2007. http://support.jnf.org/site/PageServer?pagename=Recovery

Judaism 101. Calendar. http://www.jewfaq.org/calendar.htm

Simmons, Rabbi Shraga. "Man Is a Tree." *Aish HaTorah*. http://www.aish.com/h/15sh/i/48960526.html

Torah (known as the Old Testament by Christians). Book of Leviticus.
Wein, Rabbi Berel. "Cheese and Flowers: Why Do We Eat Dairy Foods and
    Decorate the Synagogue on Shavuot?" *Aish HaTorah.* http://www.aish.
    com/h/sh/r/48967071.html#

**On the Internet**
Akhlah: Israel for Children
    http://www.akhlah.com/israel/israel.php
Dreidel Place Card How-To
    http://www.marthastewart.com/276203/dreidel-place-card?czone=entertai
    ning%2Fholiday-entertaining%2Fholidaycenter-décor
Israel4Kids: Embassy of Israel, Washington, D.C.
    http://www.israelemb.org/kids/
Judaism 101
    http://www.jewfaq.org/index.htm
Kashrut: Jewish Dietary Laws
    http://www.jewfaq.org/kashrut.htm#Links
Passover
    http://www.chabad.org/kids/article_cdo/aid/1639/jewish/The-Exodus-
    From-Egypt.htm

PHOTO CREDITS: pp. 2–3, 5, 17 (top), 25 (top), 31, 37, 57—cc-by-sa; pp. 4, 5, 8, 18, 19, 24, 48, 49, 53, 58, 60–61—
Photos.com; pp. 7, 9, 10, 11, 12, 16, 17 (bottom), 20, 21, 22, 23, 32, 33, 34, 35, 38, 39, 40, 41, 44, 45, 46, 47, 50, 51, 52, 54,
55, 59—Laya Saul; p. 14—Menahem Kahana/AFP/Getty Images; p. 15—Jack Guez/AFP/Getty Images; p. 25 (bottom), 26, 27,
28, 29—AP Photo/Ariel Schalit; p. 30—Ernest Normand; pp. 42–43—AP Photo/Sebastian Scheiner; p. 43—Gali Tibbon/AFP/
Getty Images; p. 56—Musee de la Chartreuse. Every effort has been made to locate all copyright holders of material used in this
book. If any errors or omissions have occurred, corrections will be made in future editions of the book.

# Glossary

Please note that Hebrew words are marked with their accent syllable as spoken in the United States. They may have a different accent when spoken in Israel.

**Allies** (AL-lyz)—Countries that are friendly and working together, including militarily.

**Ashkenazic** (ahsh-keh-NAH-zik)—Relating to the Jews of Eastern European descent.

**atonement** (ah-TOHN-ment)—Apologizing and making up for actions or words that damaged or injured people.

**custom** (KUS-tum)—An action that families or cultures practice at a particular time, such as during a holiday.

**exile** (EK-zyl)—To send someone away from his or her homeland.

**exodus** (EK-suh-dus)—A mass departure, such as when the Israelites left the slavery of Egypt.

**fasting** (FAS-ting)—Not eating or drinking for a certain time period.

**gragger** (GRAH-ger)—A party noisemaker that is like a ratchet.

**kashrut** (kash-ROOT)—The dietary laws as commanded in the Bible.

**kosher** (KOH-shur)—Describing foods that fall within the dietary laws.

**leaven** (LEH-ven)—To cause to rise.

**miracle** (MEER-uh-kul)—A positive event that seems to defy the laws of nature.

**mitzvah** (MITZ-vah)—Literally "commandment," or sometimes translated as "good deed"; a kindness, prayer, or blessing commanded by God; the plural is *mitzvot* (MITZ-voht).

**persecute** (PER-seh-kyoot)—To punish a person or group of people physically or by laws, especially when it is the result of one's beliefs; to lower the status of a person or nation.

**regime** (reh-JEEM)—Ruling power.

**Rosh Hashana** (RAHSH hah-SHAH-nah)—The Jewish New Year.

**Scroll** (SKROHL)—The long, rolled-up parchment on which a biblical story is written.

**Seder** (SAY-der)—From the Hebrew word meaning "order," a meal with foods eaten in a certain order or a story told in a certain order.

**Sephardic** (seh-FAR-dik)—Relating to Jews of Spanish, Asian, or Middle Eastern descent.

**Succah** (SOO-kah)—A temporary hut lived in for the holiday of Succot.

**Succot** (SOO-koht)—A harvest holiday commanded in the Bible to commemorate the dwellings of the Israelites in the desert after the Exodus.

**Torah** (TOR-ah)—The Hebrew Bible.

**tshuvah** (teh-SHOO-vah)—From the Hebrew word that means "return," to return to the truth of oneself.

**Yom Kippur** (YOHM kih-POR)—Day of Atonement, the holiest day of the Jewish year.

# Index

# ABOUT THE
# AUTHOR

Laya Saul grew up in Southern California, where she learned about Israel as a child. As a teenager, she spent a year studying and working in Israel. Then, in 2003, Laya, her husband, and their children moved to northern Israel. Her family has planted fruit trees in their yard, adopted a dog and a cat, and loves to swim in the Mediterranean Sea. She has taught Hebrew school to children and adults in the United States and has taught religious studies in Israel as well.

Laya, also known as Aunt Laya, wrote a book for teens called *You Don't Have to Learn Everything the Hard Way*. She has also written several other books for Mitchell Lane Publishers, including *We Visit Israel.*